The
Long Hidden Friend

The
Long Hidden Friend

By

John George Hohman

Edited and Illustrated by Gemma Gary

TROY BOOKS

The
Long Hidden Friend

By

John George Hohman

Edited and Illustrated by Gemma Gary

This paperback edition in introduction, editing, layout and illustrations
© Troy Books 2013

ISBN 978-1-909602-31-1

Published by Troy Books
www.troybooks.co.uk

Troy Books Publishing
BM Box 8003
London WC1N 3XX

Contents

Introduction   *6*

Original Preface   *9*

Testimonials   *11*

Curative Arts   *14*

Animal Arts   *40*

Arts Against Evildoers   *49*

Protective Arts   *56*

Propitious Arts   *68*

Introduction

The Long Hidden Friend was written by John George Hohman, and first published in German as *Der Lange Verborgene Freund* in 1820, with later translations in English, eventually receiving the title *Pow-Wows; or, Long Lost Friend*.

Hohman was a collector, practitioner and teacher of traditional magical charms, spells and herbal remedies who, in 1802, settled in the Dutch-Pennsylvania community after immigrating to America from Germany.

The name Pow-Wows may cause many who come across the book to expect its content to relate in some way to Native American tradition; pow wow being a name for Native North American gatherings.

Such readers will be surprised to find instead a collection of traditional European folk-magical formulas for a wide range of spells, simple rituals, charms, talismans, bindings, prayers and benedictions. In fact, students and practitioners of British folk magic may find many of the charms described familiar, as they are of similar character; the spoken blood-stopping charms being a notable example. A large proportion of the book is given to magical folk-healing, recipes and remedies for humans and animals. A number of non-magical 'tips' are also given for various matters of rural and domestic life.

Whilst the curative recipes and remedies contained herein will be of great historical interest to the contemporary practitioner, their use cannot be recommended, and trained medical or veterinary aid should of course be sought instead!

The contents of previous editions have tended to be rather 'rambling' and scattered, and so, in editing this edition, I have attempted to bring some sensible order to the practices described by arranging them into appropriate categories.

The later "Pow-Wows" title of this important little grimoire would seem to have been added as a result of the obsession 19th century American (and later British) Spiritualists had with Native American 'Spirit Guides'. Testament to the book's influence, the name "Pow-Wowing" became associated in Dutch Pennsylvania with a tradition of folk-magical practice perhaps more traditionally known as Braucherei, Hex, or Speilwerk, whose practitioners; the hexenmeisters, are still very active today.

JOHN GEORGE HOHMAN'S
𝕿𝖍𝖊 𝕷𝖔𝖓𝖌 𝕳𝖎𝖉𝖉𝖊𝖓 𝕱𝖗𝖎𝖊𝖓𝖉

A COLLECTION OF MYSTERIOUS AND
INVALUABLE ARTS AND REMEDIES,
FOR MAN AS WELL AS ANIMALS.

With many proofs of their virtue and efficacy in healing diseases, etc., the greatest
part which was never published until they appeared in print for the first time in
the U.S. in the year 1820.

Preface

The author would have preferred writing no preface whatever to this little book, were it not indispensably necessary, in order to meet the erroneous views some men entertain in regard to works of this character. The majority, undoubtedly, approve of the publication and sale of such books, yet some are always found who will persist in denouncing them as something wrong. This latter class I cannot help but pity, for being so far led astray; and I earnestly pray everyone who might find it in his power, to bring them from off their ways of error. It is true, whosoever taketh the name of JESUS in vain, committeth a great sin. Yet, is it not expressly written in the fiftieth Psalm, according to Luther's translation: "Call upon me in the day of trouble; I will deliver thee, and thou shalt glorify me." In the Catholic translation, the same passage is found in the forty-ninth Psalm, reading thus: "Call upon me in the day of thy trouble, and I will deliver thee, and thou shalt glorify me."

Where is the doctor who has ever cured or banished the panting or palpitation of the heart, and hide-boundness? Where is the doctor who ever banished a wheal? Where is the doctor who ever banished the mother-fits? Where is the doctor that can cure mortification when it once seizes a member of the body? All these cures, and a great many more mysterious and wonderful things are contained in this book; and its author could take an oath at any time upon the fact of his having successfully applied many of the prescriptions contained herein.

I say; any and every man who knowingly neglects using this book in saving the eye, or the leg, or any other limb of his fellow-man, is guilty of the loss of such limb, and thus commits a sin, by which he may forfeit to himself all hope of salvation. Such men refuse to call upon the Lord in their trouble, although He especially commands it. If men were not allowed to use sympathetic words, nor the name of the *Most High*, it certainly would not have been revealed to them; and what is more, the Lord would not help where they are made use of. God can in no manner be forced to intercede where it is not his divine pleasure.

Another thing I have to notice here: There are men who will say, if one has used sympathetic words in vain, the medicines of doctors could not avail any, because the words did not effect a cure. This is only the excuse of physicians; because whatever cannot be cured by sympathetic words, can much less be cured by any doctor's craft or cunning: I could name at any time that Catholic priest whose horse was cured with mere words; and I could also give the name of the man who did it. I knew the priest well; he formerly resided in Westmoreland county. If it was desired, I could also name a Reformed preacher who cured several persons of the fever, merely by writing them some tickets for that purpose; and even the names of those persons I could mention. This preacher formerly resided in Berks county. If men but use out of this book what they actually need, they surely commit no sin; yet woe unto those who are guilty that anyone loses his life in consequence of mortification, or loses a limb, or the sight of the eye! Woe unto those who misconstrue there things at the moment of danger, or who follow the ill advice of any preacher who might teach them not to mind what the Lord says in the fiftieth Psalm. "Call upon me in the day of trouble: I will deliver thee, and thou shalt glorify me." Woe unto those who, in obeying the directions of a preacher, neglect using any means offered by this book against mortification, or inflammation, or the wheal. I am willing to follow the preacher in all reasonable things, yet when I am in danger and he advises me not to use any prescriptions found in this book, in such a case I shall not obey him. And woe also unto those who use the name of the Lord in vain and for trifling purposes.

I have given many proofs of the usefulness of this book, and I could yet do it at any time. I sell my books publicly, and not secretly, as other mystical books are sold. I am willing that my books should be seen by everybody, and I shall not secrete or hide myself from any preacher. I, Hohman, too, have some knowledge of the Scriptures, and I know when to pray and call unto the Lord for assistance. The publication of books (provided they are useful and morally right) is not prohibited in the United States, as is the case in other countries where kings and despots hold tyrannical sway over the people. I place myself upon the broad platform of the liberty of the press and of conscience, in regard to this useful book, and it shall ever be my most heartfelt desire that all men might have an opportunity of using it to their good, in the name of Jesus.

Given at Rosenthal, near Reading, Berks county, Penn., on the 31st day of July, in the year of our Lord, 1819.

JOHN GEORGE HOHMAN
Author and original publisher of this book.

10

Testimonials

Which go to show at any time, that I, Hohman,
have successfully applied the prescriptions of this book:

BENJAMIN STOUDT, the Son of a Lutheran schoolmaster, at Reading, suffered dreadfully from a wheal in the eye. In a little more than 24 hours this eye was as sound as the other one, by the aid I rendered him with the help of God, in the year 1817.

HENRY JORGER, residing in Reading, brought to me a boy who suffered extreme pain, caused by a wheal in the eye, in the year 1814. In a little more than 24 hours, I, with the help of God, have healed him.

JOHN BAYER, son of Jacob Bayer, now living near Reading, had an ulcer on his leg, which gave him great pain. I attended him, and in a short time the leg was well. This was in the year 1818.

LANDLIN GOTTWALD, formerly residing in Reading, had a severe pain in his one arm. In about 24 hours I cured his arm.

CATHARINE MECK, at that time in Alsace township, suffered very much from a wheal in the eye. In a little more than 24 hours the eye was healed.

MR. SILVIS, of Reading, came to my house while engaged at the brewery of my neighbour. He felt great pain in the eye caused by a wheal. I cured his eye in a little more than 24 hours.

ANNA SNYDER, of Alsace township, had a severe pain in one of her fingers. In a little more than twenty-four hours she felt relieved.

MICHAEL HARTMAN, Jr., living in Alsace township, had a child with a very sore mouth. I attended it and in a little more than twenty-four hours it was well again.

JOHN BINGEMANN, at Ruscombmanor, Berks county, had a boy who burnt himself dreadfully. My wife came to that place in the fall of the year 1812.

Mortification had already set in - my wife had sympathy for it, and in a short time the mortification was banished. The boy was soon after perfectly cured and became well again. It was about the same time that my wife cured John Bingemann's wife of the wild-fire, which she had on a sore leg.

SUSANNA GOMBER, had a severe pain in the head. In a short time I relieved her. The wife of David Brecht also felt a severe pain in the head, and was relieved by me in a short time.

JOHN JUNKINS' daughter and daughter-in-law both suffered very much from pain in the head; and his wife too had a sore cheek, on which the wild-fire had broken out severely. The headache of the daughter and the daughter-in-law-was banished by me; and the wild-fire, of the wife was cured in some seven or nine hours. The swelled cheek burst open and healed very fast. The woman had been laid up several days already on account of it. The family of Junkins live at Nackenmixen, but Brecht and Gomber reside in and near Reading. Nackenmixen is in Bucks county. The four last mentioned were cured in the year 1819.

The daughter of John Arnold scalded herself with boiling coffee; the handle of the pot broke off while she was pouring out coffee, and the coffee ran over the arm and burnt it severely. I was present and witnessed the accident. I banished the burning; the arm did not get sore at all, and healed in a short time. This was in the year 1815. Mr. Arnold lived near Lebanon, Lebanon county, Penn.

JACOB STOUFFER, at Heckak, Bucks county, had a little child who was subject to convulsions every hour. I sold him a book containing the 25 letters; and he was persuaded by his neighbor, Henry Frankenfield, to try these 25 letters. The result was that the child was instantaneously free from convulsions and perfectly well. These letters are also to be found in this book.

☞ If any one of the above named witnesses, who have been cured by me and my wife through the help of God, dares to call me a liar, and deny having been relieved by us, although they have confessed that they have been cured by us, I shall, if it is at all possible, compel them to repeat their confession before a Justice of the Peace.

A letter to cure rheumatism, sold at from one to two dollars, and, did not even give directions how to make use of it: these depending on verbal communications. John Allgaier, of Reading, had a very sore finger. I used sympathy to banish the wild-fire and to cure the finger. The very next morning the wild-fire was gone; he scarcely felt any pain, and the finger began to heal very fast. This was in 1819.

☞ This book is partly derived from a work published by a Gypsy, and partly from secret writings, and collected with much pain and trouble, from all parts of the world, at different periods, by the author, John George Hohman. I did not wish to publish it; my wife, also, was opposed to its publication; but my compassion for my suffering fellow-men was too strong, for I had seen many a one lose his entire sight by a wheal, and his life or limb by mortification. And how dreadfully has many a woman suffered from mother-fits? And I therefore ask thee again, oh friend, male or female, is it not to my everlasting praise, that I have had such books printed? Do I not deserve the rewards of God for it? Where else is the physician that could cure these diseases? Besides that I am a poor man in needy circumstances, and it is a help to me if I can make a little money with the sale of my books.

The Lord bless the beginning and the end of this little work, and be with us, that we may not misuse it, and thus commit a heavy sin! The word misuse, means as much as to use it for anything unnecessary. God bless us! Amen. The word Amen means as much as that the Lord might bring to pass in reality what had. been asked for in prayer.

HOHMAN.

NOTE: There are many in America who believe neither in a hell nor in a heaven; but in Germany there are not so many of these persons found. I, Hohman, ask: Who can immediately banish the wheal, or mortification? I reply, and I, Hohman, say: All this is done by the Lord. Therefore, a hell and a heaven must exist; and I think very little of any one who dares deny it.

Curatíve Arts

A Certaín Remedy to stop Bleedíng

This cures, no matter how far a person be away, if only his first name is rightly pronounced while using it:

> *"Jesus Christ dearest blood!*
> *That stoppeth the pain and stoppeth the blood.*
> *In this help you (first name)*
> *God the Father, God the Son, God the Holy Ghost. Amen"*

A Second Blood-Stopping Charm

"This is the day on which the injury happened.
Blood, thou must stop, until the Virgin Mary bring forth another son".

Repeat these words three times.

A Third Blood-Stopping Charm

Count backwards from fifty inclusive till you come down to three. As soon as you arrive at three, you will be done bleeding.

A Fourth Blood-Stopping Charm

I walk through a green forest;
There I find three wells, cool and cold;
The first is called courage,
The second is called good,
And the third is called stop the blood.
✠　✠　✠

A Fifth Blood-Stopping Charm
Also to Heal Wounds in Man and Animals

On Christ's grave there grows three roses; the first is kind, the second is valued among the rulers, and the third says: blood, thou must stop, and wound, thou must heal.

Everything prescribed for man in this book is also applicable to animals.

A Sixth Charm to Stop Bleeding at Any Time

Write the name of the four principal waters of the whole world, flowing out of Paradise, on a paper, namely: *Pison, Gihon, Hedekiel and Pheat,* and put it on the wound. In the first book of Moses, the second chapter, verses 11, 12, 13, you will find them. You will find this effective.

15

A Seventh Blood-Stopping Charm

As soon as you cut yourself you must say:

"Blessed wound, blessed hour, blessed be the day on which Jesus Christ was born, in the name
✠ ✠ ✠
Amen."

An Eighth Blood-Stopping Charm

Breathe three times upon the patient, and say the Lord's Prayer three times until the words, *"upon the earth,"* and the bleeding will be stopped.

A Ninth and Still More Certain Way to Stop Bleeding

If the bleeding will not stop, or if a vein has been cut, then lay the following on it, and it will stop that hour. Yet if any one does not believe this, let him write the letters upon a knife and stab an irrational animal, and he will not be able to draw blood. And whosoever carries this about him will be safe against all his enemies.

I. m. I. K. I. B. I. P. a. x. v. ss. Ss. vas,
I. P. O. unay Lit. Dom. mper vobism.

And whenever a woman is going to give birth to a child, or is otherwise afflicted, let her have this letter about her person; it will certainly be of avail.

A Precaution Against Injuries

Whoever carries the right eye of a wolf fastened inside of his right sleeve, remains free from all injuries.

A Good Cure for Wounds

Take the bones of a calf, and burn them until they turn to powder, and then strew it into the wound. The powder prevents the flesh from putrefying, and is therefore of great importance in healing the wound.

16

How to Tie Up and Heal Wounds

Speak the following:

"This wound I tie up in three names, in order that thou mayest take from it heat, water, falling off of the flesh, swelling, and all that may be injurious about the swelling, in the name of the Holy Trinity."

This must be spoken three times; then draw a string three times around the wound, and put it under the corner of the house toward the East, and say:

"I put thee there,

✠ ✠ ✠

in order that thou mayest take unto thyself the gathered water, the swelling, and the running, and all that may be injurious about the wound. Amen."

Then repeat the Lord's Prayer and some good hymn.

To Take the Pain out of a Fresh Wound

"Our dear Lord Jesus Christ had a great many biles and wounds, and yet he never had them dressed. They did not grow old, they were not cut, nor were they ever found running. Jonas was blind, and I spoke to the heavenly child, as true as five holy wounds were inflicted."

A Salve to Heal up Wounds

Take tobacco, green or dry; if green a good handful, if dry, two ounces; together with this take a good handful of elder leaves, fry them well in butter, press it through a cloth, and you may use it in a salve. This will heal up a wound in a short time.

Or go to a white oak tree that stands pretty well isolated, and scrape off the rough bark from the eastern side of the tree; then cut off the inner bark, break it into small pieces, and boil it until all the strength is drawn out; strain it through a piece of linen, and boil it again, until it becomes as thick as tar; then take out as much as you need, and put to it an equal proportion of sheep-tallow, rosin and wax, and work them together until they form a salve. This salve you put on a piece of linen, very thinly spread, and lay it on the wound, renewing it occasionally till the wound is healed up.

Or take a handful of parsley, pound it fine, and work it to a salve with an equal proportion of fresh butter. This salve prevents mortification and heals very fast.

To Cure the Bite of a Snake

"God has created all things and they were good;
Thou only, serpent, art damned,
Cursed be thou and thy sting.
✠ ✠ ✠
Zing, zing, zing!"

A Cure for the Bite of a Mad Dog

A certain Mr. Valentine Kittering, of Dauphin County, has communicated to the Senate of Pennsylvania a sure remedy for the bite of any kind of mad animals. He says that his ancestors had already used it in Germany 250 years ago, and that he had always found it to answer the purpose, during a residence of fifty years in the United States. He only published it from motives of humanity.

This remedy consists in the weed called Chick-weed. It is a summer plant, known to the Germans and Swiss by the names of Gauchneil, Rothea Meyer, or Rother Huehnerdarm. In England it is called Red Pimpernel; and its botanical name is Angelica Phonicea. It must be gathered in June when in full bloom and dried in the shade, and then pulverized.

The dose of this for a grown person is a small tablespoonful, or in weight a drachm and a scruple, at once, in beer or water. For children the dose is the same, yet it must be administered at three different times. In applying it to animals, it must be used green, cut to pieces and mixed with bran or other feed. For the hogs the pulverized weed is made into little balls by mixing it with flour and water. It can also be put on bread and butter, or in honey, molasses, etc.

The Rev. Henry Muhlenberg says that in Germany 30 grains of this powder are given four times a day, the first day, then one dose a day for a whole week; while at the same time the wound is washed out with a decoction of the weed, and then the powder strewed in it. Mr. Kittering says that he in all instances administered but one dose, with the most happy results. This is said to be the same remedy through which the late Doctor William Stoy effected so many cures.

A Good Remedy for Bad Wounds and Burns

The word of God, the milk of Jesus' mother, and Christ's blood, is for all wounds and burnings good.
✠ ✠ ✠

It is the safest way in all these cases to make the crosses with the hand or thumb three times over the affected parts; that is to say, over all those things to which the three crosses are attached.

A Remedy for Burns

"Burn, I blow on thee!"
It must be blown on three times in the same breath, like the fire by the sun.
✠ ✠ ✠

Another to Cure a Burn

"Three holy men went out walking,
They did bless the heat and the burning;
They blessed that it might not increase;
They blessed that it might quickly cease!"
✠ ✠ ✠

A Plant Remedy for Burns

Pound or press the juice of male fern, and put it on the burnt spots and they will heal very fast. Better yet, however, if you smear the above juice upon a rag, and put it on like a plaster.

A Charm Against Burns

"Our dear Lord Jesus Christ going on a journey, saw a firebrand burning; it was Saint Lorenzo stretched out on a roast. He rendered him assistance and consolation; he lifted his divine hand and blessed the brand; he stopped it from spreading deeper and wider. Thus may the burning be blessed in the name of God the Father, Son and Holy Ghost. Amen."

19

Another Charm for Burns

"Clear out, brand, but never in; be thou cold or hot, thou must cease to burn. May God guard thy blood and thy flesh, thy marrow and thy bones, and every artery, great or small. They all shall be guarded and protected in the name of God against inflammation and mortification, in the name of God the Father, the Son, and the Holy Ghost. Amen."

A Very Good Plaster

I doubt very much whether any physician in the United States can make a plaster equal to this. It heals the white swelling, and has cured the sore leg of a woman who for eighteen years had used the prescriptions of doctors in vain.

Take two quarts of cider, one pound of bees-wax, one pound of sheep-tallow, and one pound of tobacco; boil the tobacco in the cider till the strength is out, and then strain it, and add the other articles to the liquid: stir it over a gentle fire till all is dissolved.

Another Very Good Plaster

Take wormwood, rue, medels, sheeprip-wort, pointy plantain, in equal proportions, a larger proportion of bees'-wax and tallow, and some spirits of turpentine; put it together in a pot, boil it well, and then strain it, and you have a very good plaster.

A Well-Tried Plaster to Remove Mortification

Take six hen's eggs and boil them in hot ashes until they are right hard; then take the yellow of the eggs and fry them in a gill of lard until they are quite black; then put a handful of rue with it, and afterward filter it through a cloth. When this is done add a gill of sweet oil to it. It will take most effect where the plaster for a female is prepared by a male, and the plaster for a male prepared by a female.

To Stop Pains or Smarting in a Wound

Cut three small twigs from a tree – each to be cut off in one cut – rub one end of each twig in the wound, and wrap them separately in a piece of white paper, and put them in a warm and dry place.

A Remedy to Relieve Pain

Take a rag which was tied over a wound for the first time, and put it in water together with some copperas; but do not venture to stir the copperas until you are certain of the pain having left you.

To Remove Bruises and Pains

"Bruise, thou shalt not heat;
Bruise, thou shalt not sweat;
Bruise, thou shalt not run,
No-more than Virgin Mary shall bring forth another son."
✠　✠　✠

To Remove Pain and Heal up Wounds with Three Switches

"With this switch and Christ's dear blood, I banish your pain and do you good!"
✠　✠　✠

Mind it well: you must in one cut, sever from a tree, a young branch pointing toward sunrise, and then make three pieces of it, which you successively put in the wound. Holding them in your hand, you take the one toward your right side first. Everything prescribed in this book must be used three times, even if the three crosses should not be affixed. Words are always to have an interval of half an hour, and between the second and third time should pass a whole night, except where it is otherwise directed. The above three sticks, after the end of each has been put into the wound as before directed, must be put in a piece of white paper, and placed where they will be warm and dry.

A Cure for the Headache

"Tame thou flesh and bone, like Christ in Paradise; and who will assist thee, this I tell thee
(name) for your repentance sake."
✠　✠　✠

This you must say three times, each time lasting for three minutes, and your headache will soon cease. But if your headache is caused by strong drink, or otherwise will not leave you soon, then you must repeat those words every minute. This, however, is not often necessary in regard to headache.

21

𝔄 𝔙𝔢𝔯𝔶 𝔊𝔬𝔬𝔡 𝔞𝔫𝔡 𝔖𝔞𝔣𝔢 𝔕𝔢𝔪𝔢𝔡𝔶 𝔣𝔬𝔯 𝔕𝔥𝔢𝔲𝔪𝔞𝔱𝔦𝔰𝔪

From one to two dollars have often been paid for this recipe alone, it being the best and surest remedy to cure the rheumatism. Let it be known therefore: Take a piece of cloth, some tape and thread, neither of which must ever have been in water; the thread must not have a single knot in it, and the cloth and tape must have been spun by a child not quite or at least not more than seven years of age. The letter given below must be carefully sewed in the piece of cloth, and tied around the neck, unbeshrewdly, on the first Friday in the decreasing moon; and immediately after hanging it around the neck, the Lord's prayer and the articles of faith must be repeated. What now follows must be written in the before-mentioned letter:

"May God the Father, Son and Holy Ghost grant it, Amen. Seek immediately, and seek; thus commandeth the Lord thy God, through the first man whom God did love upon earth. Seek immediately, and seek; thus commandeth the Lord thy God, through Luke, the Evangelist, and through Paul, the Apostle. Seek immediately, and seek; thus commandeth the Lord thy God, through the twelve messengers. Seek immediately, and seek; thus commandeth the Lord thy God by the first man that God might be loved. Seek immediately, and convulse; thus commandeth the Lord thy God, through the Holy Fathers, who have been made by divine and holy writ. Seek immediately, and convulse; thus commandeth the Lord thy God, through the dear and holy angels, and through his paternal and divine Omnipotence, and his heavenly confidence and endurance. Seek immediately, and convulse; thus commandeth the Lord thy God, through the burning oven which was preserved by the blessing of God. Seek immediately, and convulse; thus commandeth the Lord thy God, through all power and might, through the prophet Jonah who was preserved in the belly of the whale for three days and three nights, by the blessing of God. Seek immediately, and convulse; thus commandeth the Lord thy God, through all the power and might which proceed from divine humility, and in all-eternity; whereby no harm be done unto (N) nor unto any part of his body be they the ravenous convulsions, or the yellow convulsions, or the white convulsions, or the red convulsions, or the black convulsions, or by whatever name convulsions may be called; these all shall do no harm unto thee (N) nor unto any part of thy body, nor to thy head, nor to thy neck, nor to thy heart, nor to thy stomach, nor to any of thy veins, nor to thy arms, nor to thy legs, nor to thy eyes, nor to thy tongue, nor to any part or parcel of thy body. This I write for thee (N) in these words, and in the name of God the Father, Son and Holy Ghost. Amen. God bless it. Amen."

Notice: If anyone write such a letter for another, the Christian name of the person must be mentioned in it; as you will observe, where the N stands singly in the above letter, there must be the name.

A Very Good Remedy for the White Swelling

Take a quart of unslacked lime, and pour two parts of water on it; stir it well and let it stand over night. The scum that collects on the lime-water must be taken off, and a pint of flax-seed oil poured in, after which it must be stirred until it becomes somewhat consistent. Then put it in a pot or pan, and add a little lard and wax; melt it well, and make a plaster, and apply it to the parts affected. The plaster should be renewed every day, or at least every other day, until the swelling is gone.

A Charm Against Swellings

"Three pure virgins went out on a journey to inspect a swelling and sickness. The first one said, It is hoarse. The second said, It is not. The third said, If it is not, then will our Lord Jesus Christ come."

This must be spoken in the name of the Holy Trinity.

To Make a Good Eye-Water

Take four cents' worth of white vitriol, four cents' worth of prepared spicewort (calamus root), four cents' worth of cloves, a gill of good whiskey and a gill of water. Make the calamus fine and mix all together; then use it after it has stood a few hours.

How to Prepare Another Good Eye-Water

Take one ounce of white vitriol and one ounce of sugar of lead, dissolve them in oil of rosemary, and put it in a quart bottle, which you fill up with rose-water. Bathe the eyes with it night and morning.

A Very Good and Certain Means of Destroying the Wheal in the Eye

Take a dirty plate; if you have none, you can easily dirty one, and the person for whom you are using sympathy shall in a few minutes find the pain much relieved. You must hold that side of the plate or dish, which is used in eating, toward the eye. While you hold the plate before the eye, you must say:

"Dirty plate, I press thee,
Wheal in the eye, do flee".
✠　✠　✠

To Make an Oil out of Paper, which is Good for Sore Eyes

A man from Germany informed me that to burn two sheets of white paper would produce about three drops of oil or water, which would heal all sores in or about the eye if rubbed with it. Any affection of the eyes can be cured in this way, as long as the apple of the eye is sound.

To Remove a Scum or Skin from the Eye

Before sunrise on St. Bartholomew's Day, you must dig up four or five roots of the dandelion weed, taking good care to get the ends of the roots; then you must procure a rag and a thread that have never been in the water; the thread, which dare not have a single knot in it, is used in sewing up the roots into the rag, and the whole is then to be hung before the eye until the scum disappears. The tape by which it is fastened must never have been in the water.

A Good Remedy for the Toothache

Stir the sore tooth with a needle until it draws blood; then take a thread and soak it with this blood. Then take vinegar and flour, mix them well so as to form a paste and spread it on a rag, then wrap this rag around the root of an apple-tree, and tie it very close with the above thread, after which the root must be well covered with ground.

Another Good Remedy or the Toothache

Cut out a piece of greensward (sod) in the morning before sunrise, quite unbeshrewdly from any place, breathe three times upon it, and put it down upon the same place from which it was taken.

Yet another Cure for the Toothache

Hohman, the author of this book, has cured the severest toothache more than sixty times, with this remedy. Out of the sixty times he applied it, it failed but once in affecting a cure. Take blue vitriol and put a piece of it in the hollow tooth, yet not too much; spit out the water that collects in the mouth, and be careful to swallow none. I do not know whether it is good for teeth that are not hollow, but I should judge it would cure any kind of toothache.

For Toothache and for Deafness, Roaring or Buzzing in the Ear:

A few drops of refined camphor-oil put upon cotton, and thus applied to the aching tooth, relieves very much. When put in the ear it strengthens the hearing and removes the roaring and whizzing in the same.

To Prevent Painful Teething

A good way to cause children to cut their teeth without pain is to boil the brain of a rabbit and rub the gums of the children with it, and their teeth will grow without pain to them.

To Heal a Sore Mouth

"If you have the scurvy, or quinsy too,
I breathe my breath three times into you".
✠ ✠ ✠

𝕱or the 𝕾curby and 𝕾ore 𝕿hroat

Speak the following, and it will certainly help you:

"Job went through the land, holding his staff close in the hand, when God the Lord did meet him, and said to him: Job, what art thou grieved at? Job said: Oh God, why should I not be sad? My throat and my mouth are rotting away. Then said the Lord to Job: In yonder valley there is a well which will cure thee [name], and thy mouth, and thy throat, in the name of God the Father, the Son and the Holy Ghost. Amen."

This must be spoken three times in the morning and three times in the evening; and where it reads "which will cure", you must blow three times in the child's mouth.

𝕬 𝕽emedy 𝕱or 𝖁arious 𝖀lcers, 𝕭oils and other 𝕯efects

Take the root of an iron-weed, and tie it around the neck; it cures running ulcers; it also serves against obstructions in the bladder (stranguary), and cures the piles, if the roots are boiled in water with honey, and drank; it cleans and heals the lungs and effects a good breath. If this root is planted among grape vines or fruit trees, it promotes the growth very much. Children who carry it are educated without any difficulty, they become fond of all useful arts and sciences, and grow up joyfully and cheerfully.

𝕬 𝖁ery 𝕲ood 𝕽emedy for 𝕸ortification and 𝕴nflammation

"Sanctus Itorius res, call the rest.
Here the mother of God came to his assistance,
reaching out her snow-white hand,
against the hot and cold brand."
✠ ✠ ✠

Make three crosses with the thumb. Everything which is applied in words, must be applied three times, and an interval of several hours must intervene each time, and for the third time it is to be applied the next day, unless where it is otherwise directed.

A Very Good Remedy for the Wild-Fire

"Wild-fire and the dragon, flew over a wagon,
The wild-fire abated and the dragon skated."

To Destroy Warts

Roast chicken-feet and rub the warts with them; then bury them under the eaves.

A Very Good Remedy to Cure Sores

Boil the bulbs (roots) of the white lily in cream, and put it on the sore in the form of a plaster. Southernwort has the same effect.

To Remove a Wen During the Crescent Moon

Look over the wen, directly towards the moon, and say:

"Whatever grows, does grow
and whatever diminishes, does diminish."

This must be said three times in the same breath.

A Good Remedy for the Colic

"I warn ye, ye colic fiends!
There is one sitting in judgment, who speaketh: just or unjust.
Therefore beware, ye colic fiends!"

✠ ✠ ✠

Another Very Good Remedy for the Colic

Take half a gill of good rye whiskey, and a pipe full of tobacco; put the whiskey in a bottle, then smoke the tobacco and blow the smoke into the bottle, shake it well and drink it. This has cured the author of this book and many others. Or, take a white clay pipe which has turned blackish from smoking, pound it to a fine powder, and take it. This will have the same effect.

A Remedy for Epilepsy

This shall work provided the subject had never fallen into fire or water. Write reversedly or backwards upon a piece of paper:

IT IS ALL OVER!

This is to be written but once upon the paper; then put it in a scarlet-red cloth, and then wrap it in a piece of unbleached linen, and hang it around the neck on the first Friday of the new moon. The thread with which it is tied must also be unbleached.

✠   ✠   ✠

A Cure for the Epilepsy

Take a turtle dove, cut its throat, and let the person afflicted with epilepsy, drink the blood.

Another to Remedy Epilepsy

The following remedy for Epilepsy was published in Lancaster (Pa.) papers, in the year 1828.

TO SUFFERING HUMANITY – We ourselves know of many unfortunate beings who are afflicted with epilepsy, yet how many more may be in the country who have perhaps already spent their fortunes in seeking aid in this disease, without gaining relief. We have now been informed of a remedy which is said to be infallible, and which has been adopted by the most distinguished physicians in Europe, and has so well stood the test of repeated trials that it is now generally applied in Europe. It directs a bedroom for the sick person to be fitted up over the cow-stable, where the patient must sleep at night, and should spend the greater part of his time during the day in it. This is easily done by building a regular room over the stable. Then care is to be taken to leave an opening in the ceiling of the stable, in such a manner that the evaporation from the same can pass into the room, while, at the same time, the cow may inhale the perspiration of the sick person. In this way the animal will gradually attract the whole disease, and be affected with arthritic attacks, and when the patient has entirely lost them the cow will fall dead to the ground. The stable must not be cleaned during the operation, though fresh straw or bay may be put in; and of course, the milk of the cow, as long as she gives any, must be thrown away as useless. (Lancaster Eagle).

To Banish Convulsive Fevers

Write the following letters on a piece of white paper, sew it on a piece of linen or muslin, and bang it around the neck until the fever leaves you:

A Good Remedy for the Fever

"Good morning, dear Thursday! Take away from (name) the 77-fold fevers. Oh! thou dear
Lord Jesus Christ, take them away from him!"
✠ ✠ ✠

This must be used on Thursday for the first time, on Friday for the second time, and on Saturday for the third time; and each time thrice. The prayer of faith has also to be said each time, and not a word dare be spoken to anyone until the sun has risen. Neither dare the sick person speak to anyone till after sunrise; nor eat pork, nor drink milk, nor cross a running water, for nine days.

How to Banish the Fever

Write the following words upon a paper and wrap it up in knot-grass (breiten megrich), and then tie it upon the body of the person who has the fever:

Potmat sineat,
Potmat sineat,
Potmat sineat.

Against the Fever

Pray early in the morning, and then turn your shirt around the left sleeve, and say:

"Turn, thou, shirt, and thou, fever, do likewise turn. (Do not forget to mention the name of the person having the fever.) *This, I tell thee, for thy repentance sake, in the name of God the Father, the Son, and the Holy Ghost. Amen."*

If you repeat this for three successive mornings the fever will disappear.

A Remedy for Fever, Worms and the Colic

"Jerusalem, thou Jewish city, in which Christ our Lord, was born,
Thou shalt turn into water and blood,
Because it is for (name) fever, worms, and colic good."
✠ ✠ ✠

How to Destroy a Tape-Worm

"Worm, I conjure thee by the living God,
that thou shalt flee this blood and this flesh,
like as God the Lord will shun that judge who judges unjustly,
although he might have judged aright."

✠ ✠ ✠

A Benediction Against Worms

"Peter and Jesus went out upon the fields;
they ploughed three furrows, and ploughed up three worms.
The one was white, the other was black, and the third one was red.
Now all the worms are dead, in the name of the Father, the Son, and of the Holy Ghost."

✠ ✠ ✠

Repeat these words three times.

A Remedy for Worms, Good for Men as well as for Cattle

"Mary, God's Mother, traversed the land,
Holding three worms close in her hand;
One was white, the other was black, the third was red."

This must be repeated three times, at the same time stroking the person or animal with the hand; and at the end of each application strike the back of the person or the animal, to wit: at the first application once, at the second application twice, and at the third application three times; and then set the worms a certain time, but not less than three minutes.

A Diarrhœa Mixture

Take one ounce tinct. Rhubarb, one ounce laudanum, one ounce tinct. Cayenne pepper, one ounce spirits of camphor. Dose, from ten to thirty drops for an adult.

For Vomiting And Diarrhœa

Take pulverized cloves and eat them together with bread soaked in red wine, and you will soon find relief. The cloves may be put upon the bread.

For Dysentery and Diarrhœa

Take the moss off of trees, and boil it in red wine, and let those who are affected with those diseases drink it.

A Remedy for the Lock Jaw

We are informed by a friend that a sure preventive against this terrible disease, is, to take some soft soap and mix it with a sufficient quantity of pulverized chalk, so as to make it of the consistency of buckwheat batter; keep the chalk moistened with a fresh supply of soap until the wound begins to discharge, and the patient finds relief. Our friend stated to us that explicit confidence may be placed in what he says, that he has known several cases where this remedy has been successfully applied. So simple and valuable a remedy, within the reach of everyone, ought to be generally known. – N. Y. Evening Post.

Against Falling Away

A remedy to be used when anyone is falling away, and which has cured many persons. Let the person in perfect soberness and without having conversed with anyone, catch rain in a pot, before sunrise; boil on egg in this; bore three small holes in this egg with a needle, and carry it to an ant-hill made by big ants; and that person will feel relieved as soon as the egg is devoured.

A Remedy for Sickness

Another Remedy to be applied when anyone is sick, which has affected many a cure where doctors could not help – Let the sick person, without having conversed with anyone, put water in a bottle before sunrise, close it up tight, and put it immediately in some box or chest. Lock it and stop up the keyhole; the key must be carried one of the pockets for three days, as nobody dare have it except the person who puts the bottle with water in the chest or box.

How to Cure Weakness of the Limbs

Take the buds of the birch tree, or the inner bark of the root of the tree at the time of the budding of the birch, and make a tea of it, and drink it occasionally through the day. Yet, after having used it for two weeks, it must be discontinued for a while, before it is resorted to again; and during the two weeks of its use it is well at times to use water for a day instead of the tea.

Another Remedy for Weakness

Take Bittany and St. John's wort, and put them in good old rye whiskey. To drink some of this in the morning before having taken anything else, is very wholesome and good. A tea made of the acorns of the white oak is very good for weakness of the limbs.

A Very Good Cure for Weakness of the Limbs, for the Purification of the Blood, for the Invigoration of the Head and Heart, and to Remove Giddiness, etc:

Take two drops of oil of cloves in a tablespoonful of white wine early in the morning, and before eating anything else. This is also good for the mother-pains and the colic. The oil of cloves which you buy in the drug stores will answer the purpose. These remedies are also applicable to cure the cold when it settles in the bowels, and to stop vomiting. A few drops of this oil poured upon cotton and applied to the aching teeth, relieves the pain.

A Good Remedy for Consumption

"Consumption, I order thee out of the bones into the flesh, out of the flesh upon the skin, out of the skin into the wilds of the forest."
✠   ✠   ✠

To Banish the Whooping Cough

Cut three small bunches of hair from the crown of the head of a child that has never seen its father; sew this hair up in an unbleached rag and hang it around the neck of the child having the whooping cough. The thread with which the rag is sewed must also be unbleached.

Another for the Whooping Cough

A remedy for the whooping cough, which has cured the majority of those who have applied it – thrust the child having the whooping cough three times through a blackberry bush, without speaking or saying anything. The bush, however, must be grown fast at the two ends, and the child must be thrust through three times in the same manner, that is to say, from the same side it was thrust through in the first place.

A Good Remedy for Hysterics (or Mother Fits)

To be used three times – put that joint of the thumb which sits in the palm of the hand on the bare skin covering the small bone which stands out above the pit of the heart, and speak the following at the same time:

"Matrix, patrix,
lay thyself right and safe,
Or thou or I shall on the third day fill the grave."
✠ ✠ ✠

Another Remedy for Hysterics and for Colds

This must be attended to every evening, that is, whenever you pull off your shoes and stockings, run your finger in between all the toes and smell it. This will certainly effect a cure.

A Very Good Remedy for Palpitation of the Heart, and for Persons who are Hide-Bound

"Palpitation and hide-bound, be off (name) ribs,
Since Christ, our Lord, spoke truth with his lips."

To Destroy Crab-Lice

Take capuchin powder, mix it with hog's lard, and smear yourself with it. Or boil cammock, and wash the place where the lice keep themselves.

For the Sting of a Wasp or Bee

A Liverpool paper states as follows: "A few days ago, happening to be in the country, we witnessed the efficacy of the remedy for the sting of a wasp mentioned in one of our late papers. A little boy was stung severely and was in great torture, until an onion was applied to the part affected, when the cure was instantaneous. This important and simple remedy cannot be too generally known, and we pledge ourselves to the facts above stated."

A Very Good Remedy for the Gravel

The author of this book, John George Hohman, applied this remedy, and soon felt relieved. I knew a man who could find no relief from the medicine of any doctor; he then used the following remedy, to wit: he ate every morning seven peach-stones before tasting anything else, which relieved him very much; but as he had the gravel very bad, he was obliged to use it constantly. I, Hohman, have used it for several weeks. I still feel a touch of it now and then, yet I had it so badly that I cried out aloud every time that I had to make water. I owe a thousand thanks to God and the person who told me of this remedy.

A Good Remedy for Those who Cannot Keep their Water

Burn a hog's bladder to powder, and take it inwardly.

A Cure for Dropsy

Dropsy is a disease derived from a cold humidity, which passes through the different limbs to such a degree that it either swells the whole or a portion of them. The usual symptoms and precursors of every case of dropsy are the swelling of the feet and thighs, and then of the face; besides this the change of the natural color of the flesh into a dull white, with great thirst, loss of appetite, costiveness, sweating, throwing up of slimy substances, but little water, laziness and aversion to exercise.

Physicians know three different kinds of dropsy, which they name:

1. Anasarca, when the water penetrates between the skin and the flesh over the whole body, and all the limbs, and even about the face and swells them.

2. Ascites, when the belly and thighs swell, while the upper extremities dry up.

3. Tympanites, caused rather by wind than water. The belly swells up very hard, the navel is forced out very far, and the other members fall away. The belly becomes so much inflated that knocking against it causes a sound like that of a large drum, and from this circumstance its name is derived.

The chief thing in curing dropsy rests upon three points, namely:

1. To reduce the hardness of the swelling which may be in the bowels or other parts.

2. To endeavor to scatter the humors.

3. To endeavor to pass them off either through the stool or through the water.

The best cure therefore must chiefly consist in this: To avoid as much as possible all drinking, and use only dry victuals; to take moderate exercise, and to sweat and purge the body considerably.

If anyone feels symptoms of dropsy, or while it is yet in its first stages, let him make free use of the sugar of the herb called Fumatory, as this purifies the blood, and the Euphrasy sugar to open the bowels.

A Cure for Dropsy Said to be Infallible

Take a jug of stone or earthenware, and put four quarts of strong, healthy cider into it; take two handfuls of parsley roots and tops, cut it fine; a handful of scraped horse-radish, two tablespoonfuls of bruised mustard-seed, half an ounce of squills, and half an ounce of juniper berries; put all these in the jug, and place it near the fire for 24 hours so as to keep the cider warm, and shake it up often; then strain it through a cloth and keep it for use.

To a grown person give half a wineglassful three times a day, on an empty stomach. But if necessary you may increase the dose, although it must decrease again as soonas the water is carried off, and, as stated before, use dry victuals and exercise gently.

This remedy has cured a great many persons, and among them a woman of 70 years of age, who had the dropsy so badly that she was afraid to get out of bed, for fear her skin might burst, and who it was thought could not live but a few days. She used this remedy according to the directions given, and in less than a week the water had passed off her, the swelling of her stomach fell, and in a few weeks afterward she again enjoyed perfect health.

Or: Drink for a few days very strong Bohea tea, and eat the leaves of it. This simple means is said to have carried away the water from some persons in three or four days, and freed them from the swelling, although the disease had reached the highest pitch.

Or: Take three spoonfuls of rape-seed, and half an ounce of clean gum myrrh, put these together in a quart of good old wine, and let it stand over night in the room, keeping it well covered. Aged persons are to take two teaspoonfuls of this an hour after supper, and the same before going to bed; younger persons must diminish the quantity according to their age, and continue the use of it as long as necessary.

Or: Take young branches of spruce pine, cut them into small pieces, pour water on them and let them boil a while, then pour it into a large tub, take off your clothes, and sit down over it, covering yourself and the tub with a sheet or blanket, to prevent the vapor from escaping. When the water begins to cool let some one put in hot bricks; and when you have thus been sweating for a while, wrap the sheet or blanket close around you and go to bed with it. A repetition of this for several days will free the system from all water.

The following Valuable Recipes for Dropsy, not in the original work of Hohman, were added by the original publisher:

Make of the broom-corn seed, well powdered and sifted, one drachm. Let it steep twelve hours in a wineglass and a half of good, rich wine, and take it in the morning fasting, having first shaken it so that the whole may be swallowed. Let the patient walk after it. if able, or let him use what exercise he can without fatigue, for an hour and a half; after which let him take two ounces of olive oil, and not eat or drink anything in less than half an hour afterward. Let this be repeated every day, or once in three days, and not oftener, till a cure is effected, and do not let blood, or use any other remedy during the course.

Nothing can be more gentle and safe than the operation of this remedy. If the dropsy is in the body it discharges it by water, without any inconvenience; if it is between the skin and flesh, it causes blisters to rise on the legs, by which it will run off; but this does not happen to more than one in thirty: and in this case no plasters must be used, but apply red-cabbage leaves. It cures dropsy in pregnant women, without injury to the mother or child. It also alleviates asthma, consumption and disorders of the liver.

Advice to Pregnant Women

Pregnant women must be very careful not to use any camphor; and no camphor should be administered to those women who have the mother-fits.

Peaches

The flowers of the peach-tree, prepared like salad, opens the bowels, and is of use in the dropsy. Six or seven peeled kernels of the peach-stone, eaten daily, will ease the gravel; they are also said to prevent drunkenness, when eaten before meals.

Whoever loses his hair should pound up peach kernels; mix them with vinegar, and put them on the bald place.

The water distilled from peach flowers opens the bowels of infants and destroys their worms.

Sweet Oil

Sweet oil possesses a great many valuable properties, and it is therefore advisable for every head of a family to have it at all times about the house in order that it may be applied in cases of necessity. Here follow some of its chief virtues:

It is a sure remedy, internally as well as externally, in all cases of inflammation in men and animals.

Internally, it is given to allay the burning in the stomach caused by strong drink or by purging too severely, or by poisonous medicines. Even if pure poison has been swallowed, vomiting may be easily produced by one or two wine-glasses of sweet oil, and thus the poison will be carried off, provided it has not already been too long in the bowels; and after the vomiting, a spoonful of the oil should be taken every hour until the burning caused by the poison is entirely allayed.

Whoever is bitten by a snake, or any other poisonous animal, or by a mad dog, and immediately takes warmed sweet oil, and washes the wound with it, and then puts a rag, three or four times doubled up and well soaked with oil, on the wound every three or four hours, and drinks a couple of spoonfuls of the oil every four hours for some days, will surely find out what peculiar virtues the sweet oil possesses in regard to poisons.

In dysentery, sweet oil is likewise a very useful remedy, when the stomach has first been cleansed with rhubarb or some other suitable purgative, and then a few spoonsfuls of sweet oil should be taken every three hours. For this purpose, however, the sweet oil should have been well boiled and a little hartshorn be mixed with it. This boiled sweet oil is also serviceable in all sorts of bowel complaints and in colics; or when anyone receives internal injury as from a fall, a few spoonfuls of it should be taken every two hours; for it allays the pain, scatters the coagulated blood, prevents all inflammation and heals gently.

Externally, it is applicable in all manner of swellings; it softens, allays the pain, and prevents inflammation.

Sweet oil and white lead, ground together, makes a very good salve, which is applicable in burns and scalds This salve is also excellent against infection from poisonous weeds or waters, if it is put on the infected part as soon as it is noticed.

If sweet oil is put in a large glass, so as to fill it about one-half full, and the glass is then filled up with the flowers of the St. Johnswort, and well covered and placed in the sun for about four weeks, the oil proves then, when distilled, such a valuable remedy for all fresh wounds in men and animals, that no one can imagine its medicinal powers who has not tried it. This should at all times be found in a well-conducted household. In a similar manner, an oil may be made of white lilies, which is likewise very useful to soften hardened swellings and burns, and to cure the sore breasts of women.

Animal Arts

A Very Good Remedy to Destroy Bots or Worms in Horses

You must mention the name of the horse, and say:

"If you have any worms, I will catch you by the forehead. If they be white, brown or red, they shall and must now all be dead."

You must shake the head of the horse three times, and pass your hand over his back three times to and fro. ✠ ✠ ✠

Another Good Remedy for the Bots in Horses

Every time you use this, you must stroke the horse down with the hand three times, and lead it about three times holding its head toward the sun, saying:

"The Holy One saith: Joseph passed over a field and there he found three small worms; the one being black, another being brown, and the third being red; thou shalt die and be dead."

To Cure the Poll-Evil in Horses in Two or Three Applications

Break off three twigs from a cherry-tree: one towards morning, one towards evening, and one towards mid-night. Cut three small pieces off the hind part of your shirt, and wrap each of those twigs in one of these pieces; then clean the poll-evil with the twigs and leave them under-the eaves. The ends of the twigs which had been in the wound must be turned toward the north; after which you must do your business on them, that is to say, you must dirty them; then cover it, leaving the rags around the twigs. After all this the wound must be again stirred with the three twigs, in one or two days, and the twigs placed as before.

Another Good Remedy for the Poll-Evil in Horses

Take white turpentine, rub it over the poll-evil with your band, and then melt it with a hot iron, so that it runs into the wound. After this take neatsfoot oil or goose grease and rub it into the wound in the same manner, and for three days in succession, commencing on the last Friday of the last quarter of the moon.

For Horses that Refuse their Feed

To make horses that refuse their feed to eat again, especially applicable when they are afflicted in this manner on the public roads, open the jaws of the horse, and knock three times on his palate. This will certainly cause the horse to eat again without hesitation, and to go along willingly.

To Cure any Excrescence or Wen on a Horse

Take any bone which you accidentally find, for you dare not be looking for it, and rub the wen of the horse with it, always bearing in mind that it must be done in the decreasing moon, and the wen will certainly disappear. The bone, however, must be replaced as it was lying before.

To Cure the Sweeney in Horses

Take a piece of old bacon, and cut it into small pieces, put them in a pan and roast them well, put in a handful of fish-worms, a gill of oats and three spoonfuls of salt into it; roast the whole of this until it turns black, and then filter it through a cloth; after which you put a gill of soft soap, half a gill of rye whiskey, half a gill of vinegar, and half a pint of rain-water to it; mix it well, and smear it over the part affected with sweeny on the third, the sixth, and the ninth day of the new moon, and warm it with an oaken board.

How to Make Cattle Return to the Same Place

Pull. out three small bunches of hair, one between the horns, one from the middle of the back, and one near the tail, and make your cattle eat it in their feed.

Another Method of Making Cattle Return Home

Take a handful of salt, go upon your fields and make your cattle walk three times around the same stump or stone, each time keeping the same direction; that is to say, you must three times arrive at the same end of the stump or stone at which you started from, and then let your cattle lick the salt from the stump or stone.

Another Way to Make Cattle Return Home

Feed your cattle out of a pot or kettle used in preparing your dinner, and they will always return to your stable.

ꬍꭢr tꭞᴇ Swᴇᴌᴌɪɴg ꬴf Caᴛᴛᴌᴇ

"To Desh break no Flesh, but to Desh!"

While saying this, run your hand along the back of the animal. ✠ ✠ ✠
The hand must be put upon the bare skin in all cases of using sympathetic words.

Ꭲꬬ bᴇ Gɪᴠᴇɴ ᴛꬬ Caᴛᴛᴌᴇ Agaɪɴsᴛ Wɪᴛcꭞcraꬴᴛ

This must be written on paper and the cattle made to swallow it in their feed.

ꬍꭢr tꭞᴇ Ꭷꬬᴌᴌꬬw Ꭷꬬrɴ ɪɴ Cꬬws

Bore a small hole in the hollow horn, milk the same cow, and squirt her milk into the horn; this is the best cure. Use a syringe to squirt the milk into the horn.

How to Treat a Cow after the Milk is taken from Her

Give to the cow three spoonfuls of her last milk, and say to the spirits in her blood:

"Ninny has done it, and I have swallowed her in the name of God the Father, the Son, and the Holy Ghost. Amen."

Pray what you choose at the same time.

A Method of Treating a Sick Cow

J. The cross of Jesus Christ poured out milk;
J. The cross of Jesus Christ poured out water;
J. The cross of Jesus Christ has poured them out.

These lines must be written on three pieces of white paper; then take the milk of the sick cow and these three pieces of paper, put them in a pot, and scrape a little of the skull of a criminal; close it well, and put it over a hot fire, and the witch will have to die. If you take the three pieces of paper, with the writing on them, in your mouth and go out before your house, speak three times, and then give them to your cattle, you shall not only see all the witches, but your cattle will also get well again.

To Attach a Dog to a Person

This shall work provided nothing else was used before to effect it. Try to draw some of your blood, and let the dog eat it along with his food, and he will stay with you. Or scrape the four corners of your table while you are eating, and continue to eat with the same knife after having scraped the corners of the table. Let the dog eat those scrapings, and he will stay with you.

Security Against Mad Dogs

"Dog, hold thy nose to the ground, God has made me and thee, hound!"
✠ ✠ ✠

This you must repeat in the direction of the dog; and the three crosses you must make toward the dog, and the words must be spoken before he sees you.

To Make Chickens Lay Many Eggs

Take the dung of rabbits, pound it to powder, mix it with bran, wet the mixture till it forms lumps, and feed your chickens with it, and they will keep on laying a great many eggs.

For Good Wool Growth

A very good means to increase the growth of wool on sheep, and to prevent disease among them – William. Ellis, in his excellent work on the manner of raising sheep, relates the following: a tenant who had a flock of sheep that produced an unusual quantity of wool. He informed me that he was in the habit of washing his sheep with buttermilk just after shearing them, which was the cause of the unusual growth of wool; because it in a known fact that butter does not only improve the growth of sheep's wool, but also of the hair of other animals. Those who have no buttermilk may substitute common milk with salt and water, which will answer nearly as well to wash the sheep just sheared. And I guarantee that by rightly applying this means, you will not only have a great increase of wool, but the sheep-lice and their entire brood will be destroyed. It also cures an manner of scab and itch, and prevents them from taking cold.

A Good Method of Destroying Rats and Mice

Every time you bring grain into your barn, you must, in putting down the three first sheaves, repeat the following words: "Rats and mice, these three sheaves I give to you, in order that you may not destroy any of my wheat." The name of the kind of grain must also be mentioned.

To Destroy Field-Mice and Moles

Put unslaked lime in their holes and they will disappear.

A Good way to Destroy Worms in Bee-Hives

With very little trouble and at an expense of a quarter dollar, you can certainly free your bee-hives from worms for a whole year. Get from an apothecary store the powder called Pensses Blum, which will not injure the bees in the least. The application of it is as follows: p. 37 For one bee-hive you take as much of this powder as the point of your knife will hold, mix it with one ounce of good whiskey, and put it in a common vial; then make a hole in the bee-hive and pour it in thus mixed with the whiskey, which is sufficient for one hive at once. Make the hole so that it can be easily poured in. As said before, a quarter dollar's worth of this powder is enough for one hive.

Physic Ball for Horses

Cape aloes, from six to ten drachms; Castile soap, one drachm; spirits of wine, one drachm; syrup to form the ball. If mercurial physic be wanted, add from one-half a drachm to one drachm of calomel.

Previous to physicking a horse, and during its operation, he should be fed on bran mashes, allowed plenty of chilled water, and have exercise. Physic is always useful; it is necessary to be administered in almost every disease; it improves digestion, and gives strength to the lacteals by cleansing the intestines and unloading the liver; and if the animal is afterward properly fed, will improve his strength and condition in a remarkable degree. Physic, except in urgent cases, should he given in the morning and on an empty stomach, and, if required to be repeated, a week should intervene between each dose.

Before giving a horse a ball, see that it is not too hard nor too large. Cattle medicine is always given as a drench.

Physic for Cattle

Cape aloes, four drachms to one oz.; Epsom salts, four to six oz.; powdered ginger, three drachms. Mix and give in a quart of gruel. For calves, one-third of this will be a dose.

Sedative and Worm Ball

Powdered white hellebore, one-half drachm; linseed powder, one-half oz. If necessary, make into a ball with molasses. This ball is a specific for weed. Two ounces of gargling oil, in one-half bottle of linseed oil, is an effectual remedy for worms in horses and cattle.

Astringent for Looseness in Horses

Opium from one-half to one drachm; ginger, one and a half drachms; prepared chalk, three drachms; flour, two drachms. Powder, and make into a ball with molasses.

Mixture for Ulcers and all Foul Sores

Sulphate of zinc, one oz; corrosive sublimate, one drachm; spirit of salt, four drachms; water, one pint; mix.

Yellow Water in Horses

Take Venetian soap, juniper oil, saltpetre, sal prunella, sweet spirits of nitre, of each one ounce; make it into a ball with pulverized licorice root, and give the horse two ounces at once, and repeat if necessary. If attended with a violent fever, bleed, and give bran mashes; or, take a gallon of strong beer, or ale, add thereto two ounces of Castile soap and one ounce of saltpetre; stir, and mix daily of this with his feed. The following is also highly recommended in a German work:

Take pulverized gentian and calamus, of each one-half ounce; sulphate of potassa, two ounces; tartar emetic, liver of sulphur, and oil of turpentine, one-eighth of an ounce each; mix it with flour and water, and give the above in the incipient stage of the disease. The dose, if necessary, may be given daily for several days.

A Valuable Recipe for Galls – Windgalls in Horses

An intelligent and experienced farmer, rising of seventy years of age, residing in Allen township, Cumberland county, has assured us that the following ointment, if applied two or three times a day, will cure the most obstinate windgalls. Take one pound of the leaves of stramonium (Jamestown weed) bruised; two pounds of fresh butter or hog's lard, and one gill of the spirits of turpentine; put the whole of the ingredients into a clean earthen crock and place it with the contents over live coals for twenty or thirty minutes, stirring it occasionally: then strain it through a coarse cloth or canvas, and it forms a consistent ointment, with which anoint the windgalls two or three times a day. Fifty dollars had been offered for the above receipt, so says our informant, who kindly furnished it.

𝔚𝔦𝔫𝔡-𝔅𝔯𝔬𝔨𝔢𝔫 𝔥𝔬𝔯𝔰𝔢𝔰

The excellent ball for broken-winded horses, that has made a perfect cure of over seven hundred in less than nine months, after many other medicines being tried, in vain. Take myrrh, elecampane, and licorice root, in fine powder, three ounces each; saffron, three drachms: assafœtida, one ounce; sulphur squills and cinnabar of antimony, of each two ounces; aurum mosaicum, one ounce and a half; oil of aniseed, eighty drops. You may make it into paste with either treacle or honey, and give the horse the quantity of a hen's egg every morning for a week; and afterwards every other morning till the disorder is removed (Montague's Farrier, page 57).

Arts Against Evildoers

Against Slanderers

If you are calumniated or slandered to your very skin, to your very flesh, to your very bones, cast it back upon the false tongues.

✠   ✠   ✠

Take off your shirt, and turn it wrong side out, and then run your two thumbs along your body, close under the ribs, starting at the pit of the heart down to the thighs.

49

Against Adversities and all Manner of Contention

Power, hero, Prince of Peace, J. J. J.

A Benediction for and Against all Enemies

The cross of Christ be with me; the cross of Christ overcomes all water and every fire; the cross of Christ overcomes all weapons; the cross of Christ is a perfect sign and blessing to my soul. May Christ be with me and my body during all my life at day and at night. Now I pray, I (name), pray God the Father for the soul's sake, and I pray God the Son for the Father's sake, and I pray God the Holly Ghost for the Father's and the Son's sake, that the holy corpse of God may bless me against all evil things, words and works. The cross of Christ open unto me future bliss; the cross of Christ be with me, above me, before me, behind me, beneath me, aside of me and everywhere, and before all my enemies, visible and invisible; these all flee from me as soon as they but know or hear. Enoch and Elias, the two prophets, were never imprisoned, nor bound, nor beaten and came never out of their power; thus no one of my enemies must be able to injure or attack me in my body or my life, in the name of God the Father, the Son, and the Holy Ghost. Amen.

A Benediction Against Enemies, Sickness and Misfortune

The blessing which came from heaven, from God the Father, when the true living Son was born, be with me at all times; the blessing which God spoke over the whole human race, be with me always. The holy cross of God, as long and as broad as the one upon which God suffered his blessed, bitter tortures, bless me to-day and forever. The three holy nails which were driven through the holy hands and feet of Jesus Christ shall bless me to-day and forever. The bitter crown of thorns which was forced upon the holy head of Christ, shall bless me to-day and forever. The spear by which the holy side of Jesus was opened, shall bless me to-day and forever. The rosy blood protect me from all my enemies, and from everything which might be injurious to my body or soul or my worldly goods. Bless me, oh ye five holy wounds, in order that all my enemies may be driven away and bound, while God has encompassed all Christendom. In this shall assist me God the Father, the Son and the Holy Ghost. Amen. Thus must I (Name), be blessed as well and as valid as the cup and the wine, and the true, living bread which Jesus gave his disciples on the evening of Maunday Thursday. All those that hate you must be silent before me; their hearts are dead in regard to me; and their tongues are mute, so that they are not at all able to inflict the least injury upon me, or my house, or my premises: And likewise, all those who intend attacking and wounding me with their arms and weapons shall be defenceless, weak and conquered before me. In this shall assist me thee holy power of God, which can make all arms or weapons of no avail. All this in the name of God the Father, the Son, and the Holy Ghost. Amen.

Against the Wicked and Malicious

Here follows a charm to prevent wicked or malicious persons from doing you an injury – against whom it is of great power.

Dullix, ix, ux. Yea, you can't come over Pontio; Pontio is above Pilato.
✠ ✠ ✠

How to Relieve Persons or Animals after being Bewitched

"Three false tongues have pound thee, three holy tongues have spoken for thee. The first is God, the Father, the second is God the Son, and the third is God the Holy Ghost. They will give you blood and flesh, peace and comfort. Flesh and blood are grown upon thee, born on thee, and lost on thee. If any trample on thee with his horse, God will bless thee, and the holy Ciprian; has any woman trampled on thee, God and the body of Mary shall bless thee; if an servant has given you trouble, I bless thee through God and the laws of heaven; if any servant-maid or woman has led you astray, God and the heavenly constellations shall less thee. Heaven is above thee, the earth is beneath thee, and thou art between. I bless thee against all tramplings by horses. Our dear Lord Jesus Christ walked about in his bitter afflictions and death; and all the Jews that had spoken and promised, trembled in their falsehoods and mockery. Look, now trembleth the Son of God, as if he had the itch, said the Jews. And then spake Jesus: have not the itch and no one shall have it. Whoever will assist me to carry the cross him will I free from the itch, in the name of God the Father, the Son and the Holy Ghost. Amen."

To Release Spell-Bound Persons

"You horseman and footman, whom I here conjured at this time, you may pass on in the name of Jesus Christ, through the word of God and the will of Christ; ride ye on now and pass."

A Good Charm Against Thieves

There are three lilies standing upon the grave of the Lord our God; the first one is the courage of God, the other is the blood of God, and the third one is the will of God. Stand still, thief! No more than Jesus Christ stepped down from the cross, no more shalt thou move from this spot; this I command thee by the four evangelists and elements of heaven, there in the river, or in the shot, or in the judgment, or in the sight. Thus I conjure you by the last judgment to stand still and not to move, until I see all the stars in heaven and the sun rises again. Thus I stop by running and jumping and command it in the name of ✠ ✠ ✠. *Amen.*

This must be repeated three times.

To Still-Bind a Thief

Here follows a charm to cause male or female thieves to stand still, without being able to move backward or forward. In using any prescriptions of this book in regard to making others stand still, it is best to be walking about; and repeat the following three times:

"Oh Peter, oh Peter, borrow the power from God; what I shall bind with the bands of a Christian hand, shall be bound; all male and female thieves, be they great or small, young or old, shall be spell-bound, by the power of God, and not be able to walk forward or backward until I see them with my eyes, and give them leave with my tongue, except it be that they count for me all the stones that may be between heaven and earth, all rain-drops, all the leaves and all the grasses in the world. This I pray for the repentance of my enemies."

Repeat your articles of faith and the Lord's Prayer. If the thieves are to remain alive, the sun dare not shine upon them before their release. There are two ways of releasing them, which will be particularly stated: The first is this, that you tell them, in the name of St. John, to leave; the other is as follows: *"The words which have bound thee shall give thee free."*

Another to Spell-Bind a Thief so that He Cannot Stir

This benediction must be spoken on a Thursday morning, before sunrise and in the open air:

"Thus shall rule it, God the Father, the Son, and the Holy Ghost. Amen. Thirty-three Angels speak to each other coming to administer in company with Mary. Then spoke dear Daniel, the holy one: Trust, my dear woman, I see some thieves coming who intend stealing your dear babe; this I cannot conceal from you. Then spake our dear Lady to Saint Peter: I have bound with a band, through Christ's hand; therefore, my thieves are bound even by the hand of Christ, if they wish to steal mine own, in the house, in the chest, upon the meadow

or fields, in the woods, in the orchard, in the vineyard, or in the garden, or wherever they intend to steal. Our dear Lady said: Whoever chooses may steal; yet if anyone does steal, he shall stand like a buck, he shall stand like a stake, and shall count all the stones upon the earth, and all the stars in the heavens. Thus I give thee leave, and command every spirit to be master over every thief, by the guardianship of Saint Daniel, and by the burden of this world's goods. And the countenance shall be unto thee, that thou canst not move from the spot, as long as my tongue in the flesh shall not give thee leave. This I command thee by the Holy Virgin Mary, the Mother of God, by the power and might by which he has created heaven and earth, by the host of all the angels, and by all the saints of God the Father, the Son, and the Holy Ghost. Amen."

If you wish to set the thief free, you must tell him to leave in the name of St. John.

Another Way to Still-Bind Thieves

"Ye thieves, I conjure you, to be obedient like Jesus Christ, who obeyed his Heavenly Father unto the cross, and to stand without moving out of my sight, in the name of the Trinity. I command you by the power of God and the incarnation of Jesus Christ, not to move out of my sight,

✠　✠　✠

like Jesus Christ was standing on Jordan's stormy banks to be baptized by John. And furthermore, I conjure you, horse and rider, to stand still and not to move out of my sight, like Jesus Christ did stand when he was about to be nailed to the cross to release the fathers of the church from the bonds of hell.. Ye thieves, I bind you with the same bonds with which Jesus our Lord has bound hell; and thus ye shall be bound;

✠　✠　✠

and the same words that bind you shall also release you."

To Effect the Same in Less Time

"Thou horseman and footman, you are coming under your hats; you are scattered! With the blood of Jesus Christ, with his five holy wounds, thy barrel, thy gun, and thy pistol are bound; sabre, sword, and knife are enchanted and bound, in the name of God the Father, the Son, and the Holy Ghost. Amen."

This must be spoken three times.

To Compel a Thief to Return Stolen Goods

Early in the morning before sunrise you must go to a pear tree, and take with you three nails out of a coffin, or three horse-shoe nails that were never used, and holding these toward the rising Sun, you must say:

"Oh, thief, I bind you by the first nail, which I drive into thy skull and thy brain, to return the goods thou hast stolen to their former place; thou shalt feel as sick and as anxious to see men, and to see the place you stole from, as felt the disciple Judas after betraying Jesus. I bind thee by the other nail, which I drive into your lungs and liver, to return the stolen goods to their former place; thou shall feel as sick and as anxious to see men, and to see the place you have stolen from, as did Pilate in the fires of hell. The third nail I shall drive into thy foot, oh thief, in order that thou shalt return the stolen goods to the very same place from which thou hast stolen them. Oh, thief, I bind thee and compel thee, by the three holy nails which were driven through the hands and feet of Jesus Christ, to return the stolen goods to the very same place from which thou hast stolen them."

✠ ✠ ✠

The three nails, however, must be greased with the grease from an executed criminal or other sinful person.

Another to Recover Stolen Goods

Take good care to notice through which door the thief passed out, and cut off three small chips from the posts of that door; then take these three chips to a wagon, unbeschrewedly, however; take off one of the wheels and put the three chips into the stock of the wheel, in the three highest names, then turn the wheel backwards; and say:

Thief, thief, thief! Turn back with the stolen goods: thou art forced to do it by the Almighty power of God: ✠ ✠ ✠ God the Father calls thee back, God the son turns thee back so that thou must return, and God, the Holy Ghost leads thee back, until thou arrive at the place from which thou hast stolen. By the almighty power of God the Father thou must come; by the wisdom of God the Son thou hast neither peace nor quiet until thou hast returned the stolen goods to their former place; by the grace of God the Holy Ghost thou must ran and jump and canst find no peace or rest until thou arrivest at the place from which thou hast Stolen. God the Father binds thee, God the Son forces thee, and God the Holy Ghost turns thee back. (You must not turn the wheel too fast.) Thief, thou must come, ✠ ✠ ✠ thief, thou must come, ✠ ✠ ✠ thief, thou must come, ✠ ✠ ✠. If thou art more almighty, thief,

thief, thief; if thou art more almighty than God himself, then you may remain where you are. The ten commandments force thee, thou shalt not steal, and therefore thou must come. ✠ ✠ ✠ *Amen.*

𝕬nother to 𝕮ompel a 𝕿hief to return 𝕾tolen 𝕲oods

Walk out early in the morning before sunrise, to a juniper-tree, and bend it with the left hand toward the rising sun, while you are saying: Juniper-tree, I shall bend and squeeze thee, until the thief has returned the stolen goods to the place from which he took them. Then you must take a stone and put it on the bush, and under the bush and the stone you must place the skull of a malefactor. ✠ ✠ ✠ Yet you must be careful, in case the thief returns the stolen goods, to unloose the bush and replace the stone where it was before.

55

Protective Arts

To Prevent Bad People from Getting About the Cattle

Take wormwood, gith, five-finger weed, and assafœtida; three cents' worth of each; the straw of horse beans, some dirt swept together behind the door of the stable and a little salt. Tie these all up together with a tape, and put the bundle in a hole about the threshold over which your cattle pass in and out, and cover it well with lignum-vitæ wood. This will certainly be of use.

Against Black Witches and Evil Spirits

To prevent witches from bewitching cattle, the following is to be written and placed in the stable. Against bad men and evil spirits which nightly torment old and young people, it is to be written and placed on the bedstead.

"Trotter Head, I forbid thee my house and premises; I forbid thee my horse and cow-stable; I forbid thee my bedstead, that thou mayest not breathe upon me; breathe into some other house, until thou hast ascended every hill, until thou hast counted every fence-post, and until thou hast crossed every water. And thus dear day may come again into my house, in the name of God the Father, the Son, and the Holy Ghost. Amen."

This will certainly protect and free all persons and animals from witchcraft.

Against Evil Spirits, and all manner of Witchcraft

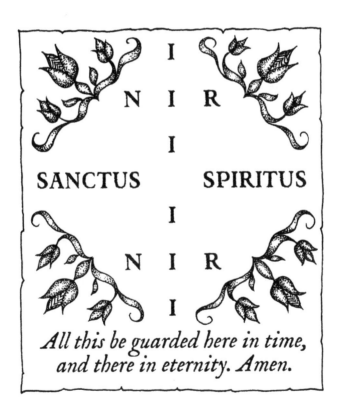

I
N I R
I
SANCTUS   SPIRITUS
I
N I R
I

All this be guarded here in time, and there in eternity. Amen.

You must write all the above on a piece of white paper and carry it about you. The characters or letters above signify: *"God bless me here in time, and there eternally."*

𝕬gainst every 𝕰vil 𝕴nfluence

"Lord Jesus, thy wounds so red will guard me against death."

𝕿o 𝕾top 𝕱ires and 𝕻estilence

Here follows a safe and approved means to be applied in cases of fire and pestilence.

"Welcome, thou fiery fiend! Do not extend further than thou already hast. This I count unto thee as a repentant act, in the name of God the Father, the Son and the Holy Ghost.
I command unto thee, fire, by the power of God, which createth and worketh everything, that thou now do cease, and not extend any further as certainly as Christ was standing on the Jordan's stormy banks, being baptized by John the holy man.
This I count unto thee as a repentant act in the name of the holy Trinity.
I command unto thee, fire, by the power of God, now to abate thy flames; as certainly as Mary retained her virginity before all ladies who retained theirs, so chaste and pure; therefore, fire, cease thy wrath.
This I count unto thee as a repentant act in the name of the holy Trinity.
I command unto thee, fire, to abate thy heat, by the precious blood of Jesus Christ, which he has shed for us, and our sins and transgressions.
This I count unto thee, fire, as a repentant act, in the name of God the Father, the Son and the Holy Ghost.
Jesus of Nazareth, a king of the Jews, help us from this dangerous fire, and guard this land and its bounds from all epidemic disease and pestilence."

Remarks: This has been discovered by a Christian Gypsy.

King of Egypt. Anno 1740, on the 10th of June, six gypsies were executed on the gallows in the kingdom of Prussia. The seventh of their party was a man of eighty years of age and was to be executed by the sword on the 16th of the same month. But fortunately for him, quite unexpectedly, a conflagration broke out, and the old Gypsy was taken to the fire to try his arts, which he successfully did to the great surprise of all present, by bespeaking the conflagration in a manner that it wholly or entirely ceased and disappeared in less than ten minutes. Upon this, the proof having been given in daytime, he received pardon and was set at liberty. This was confirmed and attested by the government of the King of Prussia, and the General Superintendent at Kœnigsberg, and given to the public in print. It was first published at Kœnigsberg in Prussia, by Alexander Bausman, Anno 1745.

Whoever has this letter fin his house will be free from all danger of fire, as well as from lightning. If a pregnant woman carries this letter about her, neither enchantment nor evil spirits can injure her or heir child. Further, if anybody has this letter in his house, or carries it about his person, he will be safe from the injuries of pestilence.

While saying these sentences, one must pass three times around the fire. This has availed in all instances.

To Prevent Conflagration

Take a black chicken, in the morning or evening, cut its head off and throw it upon the ground; cut its stomach out, yet leave it altogether; then try to get a piece of a shirt which was worn by a chaste virgin during her terms, and cut out a piece as large as a common dish from that part which is bloodiest. These two things wrap up together, then try to get an egg which was laid on maunday Thursday. These three things put together in wax; then put them in a pot holding eight quarts, and bury it under the threshold of your house, with the aid of God, and as long as there remains a single stick of your house together, no conflagration will happen. If your house should happen to be on fire already in front and behind, the fire will nevertheless do no injury to you nor to your children. This is done by the power of God, and is quite certain and infallible. If fire should break out unexpectedly, then try to get a whole shirt in which your servant-maid had her terms or a sheet on which a child was born, and throw it into the fire, wrapped up in a bundle, and without saying anything. This will certainly stop it.

A benediction to prevent fire

"The bitter sorrows and the death of our dear Lord Jesus Christ shall prevail. Fire and wind and great heat and all that is within the power of these elements, I command thee, through the Lord Jesus Christ, who has spoken to the winds and the waters, and they obeyed him. By these powerful words spoken by Jesus, I command, threaten, and inform thee, fire, flame, and heat, and your powers as elements, to flee forthwith, The holy, rosy blood of our dear Lord Jesus Christ may rule it. Thou, fire, and wind, and great heat, I command thee, as the Lord did, by his holy angels, command the great heat in the fiery oven to leave those three holy men, Shadrach and his companions, Meshach and Abednego, untouched, which was done accordingly. Thus thou shalt abate, thou fire, flame, and great heat, the Almighty God having spoken in creating. the four elements, together with heaven and earth; Fiat! Fiat! Fiat!" That is: It shall be in the name of *"God the Father, the Son, and the Holy Ghost. Amen."*

Protection of one's House and Hearth

"Beneath thy guardianship I am safe against all tempests and all enemies, J. J. J."

These three Js signify Jesus three times.

A Morning Prayer on Starting a Journey

The following is to be spoken before starting on a journey, and will save the person from all mishaps:

"I (here the name is to be pronounced) will go on a journey to-day; I will walk upon God's way, and walk where God himself did walk, and our dear Lord Jesus Christ, and our dearest Virgin with her dear little babe, with her seven rings and her true things. Oh, thou! my dear Lord Jesus Christ, I am thine own, that no dog may bite me, no wolf bite me, and no murderer secretly approach me; save me, O my God, from sudden death! I am in God's hands, and there I will bind myself. In God's hands I am by our Lord Jesus' five wounds, that any gun or other arms may not do me any more harm than the virginity of our Holy Virgin Mary was injured by the favor of her beloved Jesus." After this say three Lord's prayers, the Ave Maria, and the articles of faith.

Another Prayer on Starting a Journey

The following morning prayer is given, which is to be spoken before entering upon a journey. It protects against all manner of bad luck.

"Oh, Jesus of Nazareth, King of the Jews, yea, a King over the whole world, protect me (name) during this day and night, protect me at all times by thy five holy wounds, that I may not be seized and bound. The Holy Trinity guard me, that no gun, fire-arm, ball or lead, shall touch my body; and that they shall be weak like the tears and bloody sweat of Jesus Christ, in the name of God the Father, the Son and the Holy Ghost. Amen."

To protect Houses and Premises Against Sickness and Theft

Ito, alto Massa Dandi Bando, III. Ament
J. R. N. R. J.

"Our Lord Jesus Christ stepped into the hall, and the Jews searched him everywhere. Thus shalt those who now speak evil of me with their false tongues, and contend against me, one day bear sorrows, be silenced, dumbstruck, intimidated, and abused, forever and ever, by the glory of God. The glory of God shall assist me in this. Do thou aid me J. J. J. forever and ever. Amen."

Against Mishaps and Dangers in the House

Sanct Matheus, Sanct Marcus, Sanct Lucas, Sanct Johannis.

Against Danger and Death

To be carried about the person:

I know that my Redeemer liveth,
and that he will call me from the grave, etc.

A Peculiar Sign to Keep Back Men and Animals

Whenever you an in danger of being attacked then carry this sign with you:

"In the name of God, I make the attack. May it please my Redeemer to assist me. Upon the holy assistant of God I depend entirely; upon the holy assistance of God and my gun I rely very truly.
God alone be with us. Blessed be Jesus."

A Charm Against Powder and Ball

"The heavenly and holy trumpet blow every ball and misfortune away from me. I seek refuge beneath the tree of life which bears twelvefold fruits. I stand behind the holy altar of the Christian Church. I commend myself to the Holy Trinity. I [name] hide myself beneath the holy corpse of Jesus Christ. I commend myself unto the wounds of Jesus Christ, that the hand of no man might be able to seize me, or to bind me, or to cut me, or to throw me, or to beat me, or to overcome me in any way whatever, so help me (Name)"

Whoever carries this book with him is safe from all his enemies, visible or invisible; and whoever has this book with him cannot die without the holy corpse of Jesus

Christ, nor drown in any water, nor burn up in any fire, nor can any unjust sentence be passed upon him. So help me.

A Charm to be Carried about the Person

Carry these words about you, and nothing can hit you:

Ananiah, Azariah, and Missel, blessed be the Lord, for he has redeemed us from hell, and has saved us from death, and he has redeemed us out of the fiery furnace and has preserved us even in the midst of the fire; in the same manner may it please him the Lord that there be no fire.

I

N   I   R

I

To Charm Enemies, Robbers and Murderers

God be with you, brethren; stop, ye thieves, robbers, murderers, horsemen, and soldiers, in all humility, for we have tasted the rosy blood of Jesus. Your rifles and guns will be stopped up with the holy blood of Jesus; all swords and arms are made harmless by the five holy wounds of Jesus. There are three roses upon the heart of God; the first in beneficent, the other is omnipotent, the third is his holy will. You thieves must therefore stand under it, standing still as long as I will. In the name of God the Father, Son and Holy Ghost, you are conjured and made to stand.

A Charm Against Fire-Arms

Jesus passed over the Red Sea, and looked upon the land; and thus must break all ropes and bands, and thus must break all manner of fire-arms, rifles, guns, or pistols, and all false tongues be silenced. May the benediction of God on creating the first man always be upon me; the benediction spoken by God, when he ordered in a dream that Joseph and Mary together with Jesus should flee into Egypt, be, upon me always, and may the holy t be ever lovely and beloved in my right hand I journey through the country at large where no one is robbed, killed or murdered--where no one can do me any injury, and where not even a dog could bite me, or any other animal tear me to pieces. In all things let me be protected, as also my flesh and blood, against sins and false tongues which reach from the earth up to heaven. By the power of the four Evangelists, in the name of God the Father, God the Son, and God the Holy Ghost. Amen.

Another for the Same

I (name) *conjure ye guns, swords and knives, as well as all other kinds of arms, by the spear that pierced the side of God, and opened it so that blood and water could flow out, that ye do not injure me, a servant of God, in the ✠ ✠ ✠. I conjure ye, by Saint Stephen, who was stoned by the Virgin, that ye cannot injure me who am a servant of God, in the name of ✠ ✠ ✠. Amen.*

Protection Against all kinds of Weapons

Jesus, God and man, do thou protect me against all manner of guns, fire-arms, long or short, of any kind of metal. Keep thou thy fire, like the Virgin Mary, who kept her fire both before and after her birth. May Christ bind up all fire-arms after the manner of his having bound up himself in humility while in the flesh. Jesus, do thou render harmless all arms and weapons, like unto the husband of Mary the mother of God, he having been harmless likewise. Furthermore, do thou guard the three holy drops of blood which Christ sweated on the Mount of Olives. Jesus Christ! Do thou protect me against being killed and against burning fires. Jesus, do thou not suffer me to be killed, much less to be damned, without having received the Lord's Supper. May God the Father, Son, and Holy Ghost, assist me in this. Amen.

A Charm Against Shooting, Cutting or Thrusting

In the name of J. J. J. Amen. I (name), Jesus Christ is the true salvation; Jesus Christ governs, reigns, defeats and conquers every enemy, visible or invisible; Jesus, be thou with me at all times, forever and ever, upon all roads and ways, upon the water and the land, on the mountain and in the valley, in the house and in the yard, in the whole world wherever I am, stand, run, ride or drive; whether I sleep or wake, eat or drink, there be thou also, Lord Jesus Christ, at all times, late and early, every hour, every moment; and in all my goings in or goings out. Those five holy red wounds, oh, Lord Jesus Christ, may they guard me against all fire-arms, be they secret or public, that they cannot injure me or do me any harm whatever, in the name of ✠ ✠ ✠. May Jesus, with his guardianship and protection, shield me (name) always from daily commission of sins, worldly injuries and injustice, from contempt, from pestilence and other diseases, from fear, torture, and great suffering, from all evil intentions, from false tongues and old clatter-brains; and that no kind of fire-arms can inflict any injury to my body, do thou take care of me. ✠ ✠ ✠. And that no band of thieves nor Gypsies, highway robbers, incendiaries, witches and other evil spirits may secretly enter my house or premises, nor break in; may the dear Virgin Mary, and all children who are in heaven with God, in eternal joys, protect and guard me against them; and the glory of God the Father shall strengthen me, the wisdom of God the Son shall enlighten me, and the grace of God the Holy Ghost shall empower me from this hour unto all eternity. Amen.

To Charm Guns and Other Arms

"The blessing which came from heaven at the birth of Christ be with me (name). The blessing of God at the creation of the first man be with me; the blessing of Christ on being imprisoned, bound, lashed, crowned so dreadfully, and beaten, and dying on the cross, be with me; the blessing which the Priest spoke over the tender, joyful corpse of our Lord Jesus Christ, be with me; the constancy of the Holy Mary and all the saints of God, of the three holy kings, Caspar, Melchior and Balthasar, be with me; the holy four Evangelists, Matthew, Mark, Luke and John, be with me; the Archangels St. Michael, St. Gabriel, St. Raphael and St. Uriel, be with me; the twelve holy messengers of the Patriarchs and all the Hosts of Heaven, be with me; and the inexpressible number of all the Saints be with me. Amen."

Papa, R. tarn, Tetregammate Angen.
Jesus Nazarenus, Rex Judeorum.

A Very Effective Charm

I (name) conjure thee, sword or knife, as well as all other weapons, by that spear which pierced Jesus' side, and opened it to the gushing out of blood and water, that he keep me from injury as one of the servants of God. ✠   ✠   ✠ *Amen.*

A Very Safe and Reliable Charm

The peace of our Lord Jesus Christ be with me (name). Oh shot, stand still! In the name of the mighty prophets Agtion and Elias, and do not kill me! Oh shot, stop short. I conjure you by heaven and earth, and by the last judgment, that you do no harm unto me, a child of God. ✠   ✠   ✠

A Well-Tried Charm

Three holy drops of blood have passed down the holy cheeks of the Lord God, and these three holy drops of blood are placed before the touchhole. As surely as our dear lady was pure from all men, as surely shall no fire or smoke pass out of this barrel. Barrel, do thou give neither fire, nor flame, nor heat. Now I will walk out, because the Lord God goeth before me; God the Son is with me, and God the Holy Ghost is about me forever.

Another Well-Tried Charm Against Fire-Arms

Blessed is the hour in which Jesus Christ was born; blessed is the hour in which Jesus Christ was born; blessed is the hour in which Jesus Christ was born; blessed is the hour in which Jesus Christ has arisen from the dead; blessed are these three hours over thy gun, that no shot or ball shall fly toward me, and neither my skin, nor my hair, nor my blood, nor my flesh be injured by them, and that no kind of weapon or metal shall do me any harm, so surely as the Mother of God shall not bring forth another son. ✠ ✠ ✠. *Amen.*

A Charm to Gain Advantage of a Man of Superior Strength

I (name) breathe upon thee. Three drops of blood I take from thee: the first out of thy heart, the other out of thy liver, and the third out of thy vital powers; and in this I deprive thee of thy strength and manliness.

Hbbi Massa danti Lantien. I. I. I.

A Direction for a Gipsy Sentence

To be carried about the person as a protection under all circumstances:

Like unto the prophet Jonas, as a type of Christ, who was guarded for three days and three nights in the belly of a whale, thus shall the Almighty God, as a Father, guard and protect me from all evil. J. J. J.

To Prevent being Cheated, Charmed or Bewitched, and to be at all Times Blessed

Like unto the cup and the wine, and the holy supper, which our dear Lord Jesus Christ gave unto his dear disciples on Maunday Thursday, may the Lord Jesus guard me in daytime, and at night, that no dog may bite me, no wild beast tear me to pieces, no tree fall on me, no water rise against me, no fire-arms injure me, no weapons, no steel, no iron, cut me, no fire burn me, no false sentence fall upon me, no false tongue injure me, no rogue enrage me, and that no fiends, no witchcraft and enchantment can harm me. Amen.

Different Directions to Effect the Same

The Holy Trinity guard me, and be and remain with me on the water and upon the land, in the water or in the fields, in cities or villages, in the whole world wherever I am. The Lord Jesus Christ protect me against all my enemies, secret or public; and may the Eternal Godhead also guard me through the bitter sufferings of Jesus Christ; his holy rosy blood, shed on the cross, assist me, J. J. Jesus has been crucified, tortured and died. These are true words, and in the same way must all words be efficacious which are here put down, and spoken in prayer by me. This shall assist me that 1 shall not be imprisoned, bound or overcome by anyone. Before me all guns or other weapons shall be of no use or power. Fire-arms, hold your fire in the almighty hand of God. Thus all fire-arms shall be charmed. ✠ ✠ ✠ When the right hand of the Lord Jesus Christ was fastened to the tree, of the cross; like unto the Son of the Heavenly Father who was obedient unto death, may the Eternal Godhead protect me, by the rosy blood, by the five holy wounds on the tree of the cross; and thus must I be blessed and well protected like the cup and the wine, and the genuine true bread, which Jesus Christ gave to his disciples on the evening of Maunday Thursday. J. J. J.

Another Similar Direction

The grace of God and his benevolence he with me (N). I shall now ride or walk out; and I will gird about my loins with a sure ring. So it pleases God, the Heavenly Father, he will protect me, my flesh and blood, and all my arteries and during this day and night which I have before me; and however numerous my enemies may be, they must be dumbstruck, and all become like a dead man, white as snow, so that no one will be able to shout, cut or throw at me, or to overcome me, although he may hold rifle or steel against whomever else evil weapons and arms might be called, in his hand. My rifle shall go off like lightening, and my sword shall cut as a razor. Then wen our dear lady Mary upon a very high mountain; she looked down into a very dusky valley and beheld her dear child standing amidst the Jews, harsh, very harsh, because he was bound so harsh, because he was bound so hard; and therefore may the dear Lord Jesus Christ save me from all that is injurious to me. ✠ ✠ ✠ Amen.

And Another Similar Direction

There walk out during this day and night, that thou mayest not let any of my enemies,, or thieves, approach me, if they do not intend to bring me what was spent from the holy altar. Because God the Lord Jews is ascended into heaven in his living body. O Lord, this is good for me this day and night. ✠   ✠   ✠ *Amen.*

Another One like It

In the name of God I walk out. God the Father be with me, and God the Holy Ghost be by my side. Who ever is stronger than these three persons may approach my body and my life; yet whoso is not stronger than these three would much better let me be. J. J. J.

And Another

I conjure thee, sword, sabre or knife, that mightest injure or harm me, by the priest of all prayers, who had gone into the temple at Jerusalem, and said: An edged sword shall pierce your soul that you may not injure me, who am a child of God.

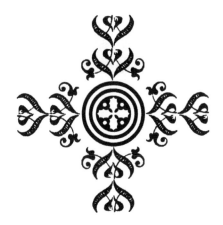

Propitious Arts

To Make a Wand for Searching for Iron, Ore or Water

On the first night of Christmas, between 11 and 12 o'clock, break off from any tree a young twig of one year's growth, in the three highest names (Father, Son, and Holy Ghost), at the same time facing toward sunrise. Whenever you apply this wand in searching for anything apply it three times. The twig must be forked, and each end of the fork must be held in one hand, so that the third and thickest part of it stands up, but do not hold it too tight. Strike the ground with the thickest end, and that which you desire will appear immediately, if there is any in the ground where you strike. The words to be spoken when the wand is thus applied are as follows:

"Archangel Gabriel, I conjure thee in the name of God, the Almighty, to tell me, is there any water here or not? Do tell me! " ✠   ✠   ✠

If you are searching for Iron or Ore, you have to say the same, only mention the name of what you are searching for.

Words to Be Spoken While Making Divinatory Wands

In making divinatory wands, they must be broken as before directed, and while breaking and before using them, the following words must be spoken:

"Divining rod, do thou keep that power,
Which God gave unto thee at the very first hour."

How to Obtain Things which are Desired

If you call upon another to ask for a favour, take care to carry a little of the five-finger grass with you, and you shall certainly obtain that you desired.

To Win Every Game One Engages In

Tie the heart of a bat with a red silken string to the right arm, and you will win every game at cards you play.

How to Walk and Step Securely in All Places

Jesus walketh with (name). He is my head; I am his limb. Therefore walketh Jesus with (name).

✠   ✠   ✠

𝔘nlucky 𝔇ays to be found in 𝔈ach 𝔐onth

January 1, 2, 3, 4, 6, 11, 12.
February 1, 17, 18.
March 14,16.
April 10, 17, 18.
May 7, 8.
June 17.
July 17, 21.
August 20, 21.
September 10, 18.
October 6.
November 6, 10.
December 6, 11, 15.

Whoever is born upon one of these days is unfortunate and suffers much poverty; and whoever takes sick on one of these days seldom recovers health; and those who engage or marry on these days become very poor and miserable. Neither is it advisable to move from one house to another, nor to travel, nor to bargain, nor to engage in a lawsuit, on one of these days.

The Signs of the Zodiac must be observed by the course of the moon, as they are daily given in common almanacs.

If a cow calves in the sign of the Virgin, the calf will not live one year; if it happens in the Scorpion, it will die much sooner; therefore no one should be weaned off in these signs, nor in the sign of the Capricorn or Aquarius, and they will be in less danger from mortal inflammation.

This is the only piece extracted from a centennial almanac imported from Germany, and there are many who believe in it. HOHMAN.

𝔄 𝔖ure 𝔚ay of 𝔆atching 𝔉ish

Take rose seed and mustard seed, and the foot of a weasel, and hang these in a net, and the fish will certainly collect there.

𝔄n 𝔈asy 𝔐ethod of 𝔆atching 𝔉ish

In a vessel of white glass must be put: 8 grains of civit, (musk), and as much castorium; two ounces of eel-fat, and 4 ounces of unsalted butter; after which the vessel must be well closed, and put in some place where it will keep moderately warm for nine or ten days, and then the composition must be well stirred with a stick until it is perfectly mixed.

APPLICATION – 1. In using the hooks.-Worms or insects used for baiting the hooks must first be moistened with this composition, and then put in a bladder or box, which may be carried in the pocket.

2. In using the net.--Small balls formed of the soft part of fresh bread must be dipped in this composition and then by means of thread fastened inside of the net before throwing it into the water.

3. Catching Fish with the hand.--Besmear your legs or boots with this composition before entering the water at the place where the fish are expected, and they will collect in great numbers around you.

A Huntsman's Talisman

It is said that anyone going out hunting and carrying it in his game-bag, cannot but shoot something worth while and bring it home.

An old hermit once found an old, lame huntsman in a forest, lying beside the road and weeping. The hermit asked him the cause of his dejection. "Ah me, thou man of God, I am a poor, unfortunate being; I must annually furnish my lord with as many deer, and hares, and partridges, as a young and healthy huntsman could hunt up, or else I will be discharged from my office; now I am old and lame; besides game is getting scarce, and I cannot follow it up as I ought to; and I know not whit will become of me." Here the old man's feelings overcame him, and he could not utter another word. The hermit, upon this, took out a small piece of paper, upon which he wrote some words with a pencil, and handing it to the huntsman, he said: "there, old friend, put this in your game-bag whenever you go out hunting, and you shall certainly shoot something worth while, and bring it home, too; yet be careful to shoot no more than you necessarily need, nor to communicate it to anyone that might misuse it, on account of the high meaning contained in these words." The hermit then went on his journey, and after a little the huntsman also arose, and without thinking of anything in particular he went into the woods, and had scarcely advanced a hundred yards when he shot as fine a roebuck as he ever saw in his life.

This huntsman was afterward and during his whole lifetime lucky in his hunting, so much so that he was considered one of the best hunters in that whole country. The following is what the hermit wrote on the paper:

Ut nemo in sense tentat, descendre nemo.

At precedenti spectatur mantica tergo.

The best argument is to try it.

To Prevent Anyone from Killing Game

Pronounce the name, as for instance; *"Jacob Wohlgemuth, shoot whatever you please; shoot but hair and feathers with and what you give to poor people.* ✠   ✠   ✠ *Amen."*

For Gaining a Lawful Suit

If anyone has to settle any just claim by way of a law suit let him take some of the largest kind of sage and write the name of the twelve apostles on the leaves, and put them in his shoes before entering the courthouse, and he shall certainly gain the suit.

To Retain the Right in Court and Council

Jesus Nazarenus, Rex Judeorum

First carry these characters with you, written on paper, and then repeat the following words: *"I* (name) *appear before the house of the Judge. Three dead men look out of the window;*

one having no tongue, the other having no lungs, and the third was sick, blind and dumb." This is intended to be used when you are standing before a court in your right, and the judge not being favorably disposed toward you. While on your way to the court you must repeat the benediction already given above.

To Extinguish Fire Without Water

Write the following words on each side of a plate, and throw it into the fire, and it will be extinguished forthwith:

Another Method of Stopping Fire

"Our dear Sarah journeyed through the land, having a fiery hot brand in her hand. The fiery brand heats; the fiery brand sweats. Fiery brand, stop your beat; fiery brand, stop your sweat."

How to Fasten or Spell-Bind Anything

You say, *"Christ's cross and Christ's crown, Christ Jesus' colored blood, be thou every hour good. God, the Father, is before me; God, the Son, is beside me; God, the Holy Ghost, is behind me. Whoever now is stronger than these three persons may come, by day or night, to attack me."* ✠ ✠ ✠
Then say the Lord's prayer three times.

Another Way of Fastening or Spell-Binding

After repeating the above, You speak:

"At every step may Jesus walk with (name). He is my head; I am his limb; therefore, Jesus, be with (name)."

A Benediction for all Purposes

"Jesus, I will arise; Jesus, do thou accompany me; Jesus, do thou lock my heart into thine, and let my body and my soul be commended unto thee. The Lord is crucified. May God guard my senses that evil spirits may not overcome me, in the name of God the Father, Son, and the Holy Ghost. Amen."

A Remarkable Passage from the Book of Albertus Magnus

It says: If you burn a large frog to ashes, and mix the ashes with water, you will obtain an ointment that will, if put on any place covered with hair, destroy the hair and prevent it from growing again.

Another Passage from the Work of Albertus Magnus

If you find the stone which a vulture has in his knees, and which you may find by looking sharp, and put it in the victuals of two persons who hate each other, it causes them to make up and be good friends.

A Recipe for Destroying Spring-Tails or Ground-Fleas

Take the chaff upon which children have been lying in their cradles, or take the dung of horses, and put that upon the field, and the spring-tails or ground-flees will no longer do you any injury.

To Prevent the Hessian Fly from Injuring the Wheat

Take pulverized charcoal, make ley of it, and soak the seed wheat in it; take it out of the ley, and on every bushel of wheat sprinkle a quart of urine; stir it well, then spread it out to dry.

To Prevent Cherries from Ripening Before Martinmas

Engraft the twigs upon a mulberry-tree, and your desire is accomplished.

Stinging Nettles

Good for banishing fears and fancies, and to cause fish to collect. Whenever you hold this weed in your hand together with Millifolia, you are safe from all fears and fancies that frequently deceive men. If you mix it with a decoction of the hemlock, and rub your hands with it, and put the rest in water that contains fish, you will find the fish to collect around your hands. Whenever you pull your hands out of the water, the fish disappear by returning to their former places.

Heliotrope (Sun-Flower) a Means to Prevent Calumniation

The virtues of this plant are miraculous. If it be collected in the sign of the lion, in the month of August, and wrapped up in a laurel leaf together with the tooth of a wolf. Whoever carries this about him, will never be addressed harshly by anyone, but all will speak to him kindly and peaceably. And if anything has been stolen from you put this under your head during the night, and you will surely see the whole figure of the thief. This has been found true.

Swallow-Wort

A means to overcome and end all fighting and anger, and to cause a sick man to weep when his health is restored, or to sing with a cheerful voice when on his death bed; also a very good remedy for dim eyes or shining of the eyes. This weed grows at the time when the swallows build their nests or eagles breed. If a man carries this' about him, together with the heart of a mole, he shall overcome all fighting and anger. If these things . are put upon the head of a sick man, he shall weep at the restoration of his health, and sing with a cheerful voice when he comes to die. When the swallow-wort blooms, the flowers must be pounded up and boiled, and then the water must be poured off into another vessel, and again be placed to the fire and carefully skimmed; then it must be filtered through a cloth and preserved, and whosoever has dim eyes or shining eyes, may bathe his eyes with it, and they will become clear and sound.

How to Make Molasses

Take pumpkins, boil them, press the juice out of them, and boil the juice to a proper consistence. There is nothing else necessary. The author of this book, John George Hohman has tasted this molasses, thinking it was the genuine kind, until the people of the house told him what it was.

To Mend Broken Glass

Take common cheese and wash it well, unslaked lime and the white of eggs, rub all these well together until it becomes one mass, and then use it. If it is made right, it will certainly hold.

To Make Good Beer

Take a handful of hops, five or six gallons of water, about three tablespoonfuls of ginger, half a gallon of molasses; filter the water, hops and ginger into a tub containing the molasses.

To Prevent the Worst Kind of Paper from Blotting

Dissolve alum in water, and put it on the paper, and I, Hohman, would like to see who cannot write on it, when it is dried.

Recipe for Making a Paste to Prevent Gun-Barrels from Rusting, whether Iron or Steel

Take an ounce of bear's fat, half an ounce of badger's grease, half an ounce of snake's fat, one ounce of almond oil, and a quarter of an ounce of pulverized indigo, and melt it altogether in a new vessel over a fire, stir it well, and put it afterward into some vessel. In using it, a lump as large as a common nut must be put upon a piece of woollen cloth and then rubbed on the barrel and lock of the gun, and it will keep the barrel from rusting.

To Make a Wick which is Never Consumed

Take an ounce of asbestos and boil it in a quart of strong lye for two hours; then pour off the lye and clarify what remains by pouring rain-water on it three or four times, after which you can form a wick from it which will never be consumed by the fire.

Soap Powders

Take one pound of hard soap, cut it fine, and mix with it one pound of soda ash. This article is much used, and its preparation, we believe, is a "great secret."

Making Dyes - To Dye a Madder Red

For each pound of cloth, soak half a pound of madder in a brass kettle over night, with sufficient warm water to cover the cloth you intend to dye. Next morning put in two ounces of madder compound for every pound of madder. Wet your cloth and wring it out in clean water, then put it into the dye. Place the kettle over the fire, and bring it slowly to a scalding heat, which will take about half an hour; keep at this heat half an hour, if a light red is wanted, and longer if a dark one, the color depending on the time it remains in the dye. When you have obtained the color, rinse the cloth immediately in cold water.

To Dye a Fine Scarlet Red

Bring to a boiling heat, in a brass kettle, sufficient soft water to cover the cloth you wish to dye; then add 11/2 oz. cream of tartar for every pound of cloth. Boil a minute or two, add two oz. lac dye and one oz. madder compound (both previously mixed in an earthen bowl), boil five minutes; now wet the cloth in warm water and wring it out and put it into the dye; boil the whole nearly an hour, take the cloth out and rinse it in clear cold water.

To Dye a Permanent Blue

Boil the cloth in a brass kettle for an hour, in a solution containing five parts of alum and three of tartar for every 32 parts of cloth. It is then to be thrown into warm water, previously mixed with a greater or less proportion of chemic blue, according to the shade the cloth is intended to receive. In this water it must be boiled until it has acquired the desired color.

To Dye a Green

For every pound of cloth add 31/2 oz. of alum and one pound of fustic. Steep (not boil) till the strength is out; soak the cloth till it acquires a good yellow, then remove the chips, and add the chemic blue by degrees till you have the desired color.

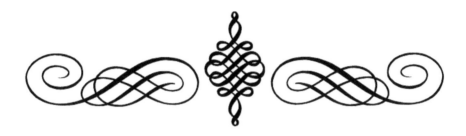

Whoever carries this book with him, is safe from all his enemies, visible or invisible; and whoever has this book with him cannot die without the holy corpse of Jesus Christ, nor drowned in any water, nor burn up in any fire, nor can any unjust sentence be passed upon him. So help me.

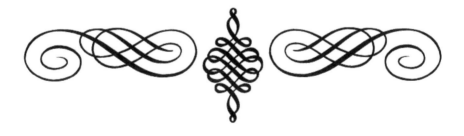

9 781909 602311